WITHDRAWN

WILD AMERICA

TURTLES

By Lee Jacobs

BLACKBIRCH®
PRESS

THOMSON

GALE

San Diego • Detroit • New York • San Francisco • Cleveland • New Haven, Conn. • Waterville, Maine • London • Munich

For more information, contact
The Gale Group, Inc.
27500 Drake Rd.
Farmington Hills, MI 48331-3535
Or you can visit our Internet site at http://www.gale.com

Photo Credits: Cover, page 10 © PhotoDisc; back cover, pages 3, 5, 6-7, 12-13, 15, 16-17 © Corel Corporation; pages 4, 14 © Thomas Kitchin and Victoria Hurst, pages 8-9, 18, 19, 20, 21, 22, 23 © CORBIS; page 11 © John White

LIBRARY OF CONGRESS CATALOGING-IN-PUBLICATION DATA

Jacobs, Lee.
  Turtles / by Lee Jacobs.
     v. cm. — (Wild America)
  Contents: The turtle's environment — The turtle body — Behavior — Hunters and gatherers — Mating game — Turtles and humans.
  ISBN 1-56711-571-3 (hardback : alk. paper)
  1. Turtles—Juvenile literature. [1. Turtles.] I. Title.

QL666.C5 J33 2003
597.92—dc21   2002012531

Printed in China
10 9 8 7 6 5 4 3 2 1

Contents

Introduction

Turtles are one of the world's oldest species. They roamed the earth before dinosaurs did! Turtles are part of a group of animals called reptiles. Reptiles are cold-blooded animals. That means that the temperature of their blood changes with the temperature of the environment around them. To warm their bodies, they stay in the sun. To cool down, they find shade or go into water. Reptiles also have protective coverings on their bodies, such as scales or plates. And most reptiles hatch from eggs.

A turtle warms itself in the sun. A turtle's body temperature changes with the temperature of its environment.

Turtles make up the order Testudines. There are more than 260 species of turtles in the world. They live on every continent except Antarctica. There are three main groups of turtles—sea turtles, freshwater turtles, and land-dwelling turtles. (The word *tortoise* is sometimes used to describe turtles that live strictly on land.) As their name suggests, sea turtles live in the world's seas and oceans. For example, loggerhead and leatherback turtles are both found along the coasts of the United States and parts of Canada.

Freshwater turtles spend time both on land and in the water. Some common North American freshwater turtles include mud, painted, box, musk, snapping, and softshell turtles. Edible (good to eat) freshwater turtles are also called terrapins. These include the diamondback terrapins that live along the eastern and southern coasts of America.

The sea turtle (left) lives in oceans and seas, while the desert tortoise (right) lives only on land.

The Turtle's Environment

Turtles are able to live in a wide variety of environments. This is one of the reasons they have been able to survive on earth for so long. They are found in wetlands, forests, deserts, and oceans. Most freshwater turtles live both in and out of water. They can live in any place that has lakes, rivers, streams, swamps, or other bodies of water.

On land, many freshwater turtles make resting spots in hollow logs, soft pine needles, or in the dirt. In the water, they burrow in mud or under rocks or old tree stumps. Snapping turtles like to take over abandoned muskrat lodges.

A mud turtle can live in lakes, rivers, or streams.

Tortoises live only on land. They prefer dry, sandy areas. The gopher tortoise works throughout its life on a burrow that it begins to dig when it is young. These burrows can reach more than 12 feet (4 m) into the ground and be as long as 30 feet (9 m). Gopher tortoises often share their burrows peacefully with other animals such as raccoons, rabbits, and opossums. A gopher tortoise's burrow may even be home to a rattlesnake!

Freshwater and land-dwelling turtles that live in colder climates hibernate (sleep through the winter). Different species do this in different ways. They may burrow into river bottoms, make small holes in the ground, or bury themselves in mud. During hibernation, turtles do not eat. Instead, they live off the fat stored in their bodies.

A California desert tortoise blends in with the dirt. Tortoises prefer to live in dry, sandy areas.

The Turtle Body

The most striking thing about a turtle's body is its shell. Turtle shells most often come in shades of brown or green, but they can also have many beautiful colors and markings. Their hard shells protect most turtles from predators (animals that hunt other animals for food).

Turtles have many predators, such as foxes, raccoons, dogs, birds, and even humans. To protect itself, the first thing a turtle often does is pull its head, legs, and tail inside its shell. This handy hiding spot travels with the turtle at all times! A tortoise might also duck into a nearby hole or burrow, while a freshwater turtle may slip into the water to hide.

A turtle's shell is made of bone. It has two main parts. The top of the shell is called the carapace. The bottom is called the plastron. The carapace and plastron are joined together by a bridge.

A turtle shell can protect a turtle from predators.
Opposite page: The carapace (top) and plastron (bottom) of a turtle shell.

The openings in the bridge are where the legs, tail, and head stick out. Box and mud turtles can close their shells tighter than any other turtles. When one of these turtles seals its bridge, nothing can get through until the turtle decides to open up again. A turtle's shell also has a hard covering with scaly plates, or scutes. This covering protects the shell and often has markings and colors that help a turtle blend in with its surroundings.

Sea turtles have flatter and more flexible shells than other types of turtles. Because of this, sea turtles can only pull their heads slightly into their shells. Leatherback sea turtles get their name from their special shell. Instead of the hard shell that other turtles have, a leatherback is covered with leathery skin. The softshell turtle also lacks a hard shell.

Turtles range widely in size. Mud and musk turtles can be less than 4 inches (10 cm) long, while leatherback sea turtles are huge. In fact, sea turtles are the largest turtles in the world.

The leatherback can weigh more than 1,000 pounds (454 kg) and stretch more than 8 feet (2 m) in length! Loggerhead turtles are also much bigger than North America's freshwater turtles. Loggerheads average between 3 and 4 feet (0.9 to 1.2 m) in length and can weigh more than 400 pounds (182 kg).

Many of the turtle species common in North America are between 4 and 10 inches (10 and 25 cm) long. Snapping turtles tend to be a bit larger. They average from 8 to 20 inches (20 to 51 cm) in length. Gopher tortoises and softshell turtles can reach lengths of 15 to 24 inches (38 to 61 cm).

Freshwater turtles and tortoises have strong, sturdy legs that can carry their heavy shells. The claws on their feet help them tear food apart. Turtles that spend much of their time in the water have webbed feet.

Sea turtles have flippers instead of legs. They use them to swim swiftly through the water. Some sea turtles can move as fast as 20 miles (32 km) per hour. Sea turtles swim great distances. They can cover thousands of miles during their lives.

Turtles have short tails, although the tails of males are usually a bit longer than those of females. Turtles do not have teeth. Instead, they have a sharp, hooked beak and extremely strong jaws that are lined with horny ridges. With these tools, turtles can deliver a powerful bite that can hurt a predator or crunch up prey.

Turtles have very good eyesight. Not only can they see distant objects move, but they can also see in color. Sea turtles cannot see well on land during the day. At night, though, they can actually see better on land than other turtle species. This helps female sea turtles during times when they come on shore to lay their eggs. Sea turtles can see very well underwater.

All turtles also have an excellent sense of smell. Although they do not have external ears, they can feel the vibrations of sound. They also have a well-developed sense of touch in their tails, feet, and shell covering. All of these sharp senses help turtles detect danger and find food.

A sea turtle uses its flippers to swim. Sea turtles can swim as fast as 20 miles (32 km) per hour.

Behavior

Turtles most often duck into their shells if a larger animal is nearby. But some species can get quite fierce when they have to defend themselves. The snapping turtle will usually hide if it is disturbed in the water. If a person swims too close and pesters it, though, a snapping turtle will snap, hiss, and snort. And on land, these turtles can get very snappy if they are bothered!

A snapping turtle
will fiercely
defend itself.

Softshell turtles are not afraid of people, either. They will bite if annoyed. Gopher tortoises are the tamest turtles. Even so, they will bob their heads up and down to show a fellow turtle that they are in charge. Musk turtles have another line of defense. Like a skunk, a musk turtle has scent glands that give off a powerful stink when the turtle is threatened.

Though a softshell turtle is not afraid of people, it will bite if it is bothered.

Hunters and Gatherers

Turtles mainly eat plant food, but most turtles eat both plants and animals. Animal foods include insects, snails, fish, tadpoles, and worms. Mushrooms and fruit are common plant foods. Some species, such as the box turtle, will kill several worms at once and then eat them at a leisurely pace.

Snapping turtles eat more kinds of food than many other types of turtles. Common snapping turtles chase their prey, sometimes right out of the water and onto land. In addition to the usual turtle food, they will eat birds, muskrats, frogs, and snakes. Snapping turtles have even been known to raid chicken coops!

A common snapping turtle will eat snakes as well as plants and insects.

Alligator snapping turtles stay well hidden on river bottoms. There, they wait for prey to swim nearby. Then, as their name suggests, they quickly snap up their dinner, just as an alligator might do. Land turtles such as gopher tortoises like fruit, leaves, and flowers. Sea turtles eat fish, sea plants, shellfish, and jellyfish.

The Mating Game

The breeding season for most types of turtles begins in the spring. Many North American turtles lay eggs once a year, although the diamondback terrapin deposits a clutch (group of eggs) up to 5 times a year. Nests are always built on land. The female digs a hole in the ground where she lays her round, white eggs.

The number and size of eggs in a clutch vary with different species. In general, smaller turtles lay fewer eggs than larger turtles. Mud turtles lay 3 to 5 eggs, snapping turtles lay 20 to 30, and sea turtles lay about 100.

A female sea turtle digs a hole in which to bury her eggs. Most North American turtles lay eggs once a year.

18

After she lays her clutch in the nest, the female covers the eggs with dirt or sand. This protects them from the weather and from animals that like to eat turtle eggs, such as raccoons, foxes, and coyotes. Once the clutch is covered, the female leaves the nest behind. She does not come back to raise her young.

Unlike other kinds of turtles, sea turtles breed 5 or 6 times in a year. Then, they usually wait a few years before they mate again. Sea turtles spend most of their lives in the ocean. When they are ready to mate, though, they leave the deep sea and swim near the shore. Males rarely leave the water, and females go ashore only when it is time to make a nest and lay their eggs.

Because sea turtles are so heavy, it is hard for them to move on land. The female uses her front flippers to pull herself slowly along until she reaches dry sand. Then she uses her rear flippers to dig a hole that will serve as a nest. Throughout the breeding season, a female stays in the waters close to her beach, and returns to land each time she is ready to dig a new nest and lay a clutch of eggs. Females often travel hundreds of miles to make their nests on the same beach where they were born.

A female sea turtle makes her way back to the sea after laying her eggs in the sand.

Hatchlings

In their warm nests, baby turtles grow inside their eggs for 2 to 3 months. From each nest, either male or female turtles—not both—will emerge at hatching time. This is because the temperature of the nest determines the sex of the hatchlings, or baby turtles. Males tend to develop in nests that are a few degrees cooler than those that produce female hatchlings.

Hatchlings have a sharp egg tooth that they use to crack their eggs when they are ready to break free. It can take a few days for a baby to split its egg open and wriggle out. Once the hatchling is a few weeks old, the egg tooth falls off, since it is no longer needed.

Not much is known about turtles in their first year of life because they are so skilled at staying hidden to avoid predators.

A hatchling uses its egg tooth to crack its egg. It can take the hatchling a few days to get completely out of its shell.

All baby turtles are in danger of predator attack because their shells are very soft. Birds, crabs, dogs, raccoons, foxes, and other animals will eat baby turtles. But hatchlings know how to seek safety. They scurry off to find leaves or other brush to hide in.

Sea turtles are born as close to the shore as they can be without being in danger of having their nest flooded by the incoming tide. They waddle into the ocean as fast as they can. Many do not make it. Seagulls and crabs snatch them up before they reach the sea. Even if they do make it to the water, the hatchlings still face the danger that fish will eat them. Hatchlings that survive, though, can live a long time. In fact, turtles have a longer life span than any other animal. Some species can live well over 100 years.

On land, a hatchling's main source of food is insects. As they get older, they will eat a wider variety of plant and other foods. Baby sea turtles mainly eat plankton. As they grow, they begin to eat fish, small crabs, and shrimp.

Turtles and Humans

Turtles have always fascinated people. Turtles appear in the myths of many cultures and are often thought to be wise. But turtles have also suffered greatly because of humans. Turtle shells have been used to make jewelry and other decorative objects. Turtles are taken from the wild and kept as pets. Sea turtles drown if they get caught in the nets used to catch shrimp and fish. Crowded beaches invade turtle nesting sites. Many people also eat turtle meat and turtle eggs. The number of gopher tortoises and diamondback terrapins in the United States has gone down because of this practice.

People try to help turtles by taking turtle eggs from a nesting site to a place where they can hatch safely.

In addition, turtle habitats are destroyed by land development and pollution. Many turtle species are now endangered, which means that there is a risk that they will be wiped out. In fact, all species of sea turtles are already endangered. Some steps have been taken to protect turtles. For example, people are kept off beaches during turtle nesting times. More efforts are still needed, however, to protect the turtles of the world.

Researchers measure a leatherback turtle. Information gathered from nesting sites is used to teach people about the importance of turtles.

23

Glossary

bridge the part of a turtle's shell that joins the top and bottom halves together

carapace the top of a turtle's shell

clutch a group of turtle eggs laid at one time

hatchlings baby turtles

hibernate to sleep through the winter

plastron the bottom of a turtle's shell

predator an animal that hunts another animal for food

scutes the scaly covering of a turtle's shell

For Further Reading

Arnosky, Jim. *All About Turtles*. New York: Scholastic Press, 2000.

Berger, Melvin. *Look Out for Turtles!* New York: HarperCollins, 1992.

Gibbons, Gail. *Sea Turtles*. New York: Holiday House, 1998.

Kalman, Bobbie. *What is a Reptile?* New York: Crabtree Publishing, 1999.

Index